Do You Know Enough About Me To Teach Me?

A Student's Perspective

Stephen G. Peters

Second Edition

The Peters Group Foundation, 2006

For information on permissions to reprint sections of this book, for a complete list of training programs, or to arrange speaking engagements, please contact The Stephen Peters Group at www.stephenpetersgroup.com.

Book revision and editing services by CaseNEX LLC.
Composition and design by Optipop Design & Marketing.
Manufacturing by King Lindsay Printing Corp.

Peters, Stephen G.
Do you know enough about me to teach me?
A Student's Perspective / Stephen G. Peters

ISBN 0-9790028-0-x
Formerly published as ISBN 0-944514-92-8

The Peters Group Foundation, 2868 Columbia Road, Orangeburg, S.C. 29118

This book is dedicated to the cherished memory of my mother Charity and brother Clint—and also, to all of the young children and teachers in America who understand or will understand that "freedom" comes only through education.

Contents

Preface

I HAVE BEEN in the education field for more than twenty-five years as a classroom teacher, assistant principal, principal, and director of secondary education. Most of my experiences have been in schools that have shown significant growth over short periods of time, gaining national and state "Blue Ribbon" distinction.

After founding "The Gentlemen's Clubs," a fast-growing program that has been highly successful in changing attitudes and behavior among at-risk and borderline males, I found that I had become a national education expert, serving on panels with the likes of former U.S. Secretary of Education Dr. Ronald Paige and appearing on television programs with a global reach, such as *America, America* and *The Oprah Winfrey Show*.

None of this would have been possible without God and my family. I thank God for His anointing and the many blessings He has bestowed upon me. I thank my wife, Angela, who inspires me, and I thank our children—Jillian, Jourdan, Xavier, and Maya—for understanding the demands of hard work in service to mankind. I thank my father, Nathaniel, for giving me life and encouragement.

I am also grateful to Judy Cubbison and Brandi Waymer of the Peters Group and to our partners at CaseNEX in Charlottesville, Virginia, for helping us to "polish this diamond" and reach educators all over the world who are casting about for help.

Finally, I thank my extended family—both those of my blood, who have always been there for me, and those of my heart and intellect at Visionary Leaders Institute in Columbus, Ohio.

Stephen G. Peters

Introduction

IMAGINE walking into the Doctor's office and having the Doctor prescribe medication for you without asking any questions or forcing you to fill out one of those lengthy medical history questionnaires. You can't, can you? But daily, hundreds of thousands of our children are being subjected to this treatment. Teachers who know little of their lives are teaching them in ways they don't understand, which makes it almost impossible for them to grasp concepts and for the teachers to transfer knowledge. This is difficult and frustrating both for students who have a desire to learn and for teachers who have a sincere desire to teach.

While teachers must pay close attention to where they are in terms of page number or content, it makes very little sense to continue with a goal of covering page after page, chapter after chapter, of material while the children are failing to understand the material covered. Curriculum specialists maintain we must make sure this material is covered in a specified period of time. But I empathize with teachers who are in an impossible bind: doing and trying everything possible for their children but still coming up short.

"Do You Know Enough About Me to Teach Me?" A Student's Perspective offers its readers an opportunity to affirm and validate those approaches and strategies they are already using successfully even as it makes it possible to accept the reality that today's students need more.

As a teacher, my gift was the ability to capture and inspire my students. As an administrator, I was able to do the same with my teachers and staff. Now, as an author, I want to *capture* and *inspire* you, the reader, to understand and embrace the power and authority you have within you to build up children and encourage their dreams or tear them down.

There are so many problems facing public education today. They are too numerous to name. I am a firm believer that the answers to many of these problems or issues rest within the hearts and minds of our young people and that everyone loses when we silence or ignore their voices.

"Do You know Enough About Me To Teach Me?" captures these voices through conversations I have had and formal interviews I have conducted over the years. The snapshot of our nation's youth that emerges shows them to be by turns engaging, confused, intelligent, focused, and concerned as they share their viewpoints about our schools, classrooms, and communities. In addition, they give clear examples of the many obstacles that stand in their way as we teachers strive to develop their abilities.

Nobody rises to low expectations! Let us all remember our own experiences in school and make an attempt to transfer the great moments to those we are called to educate and cancel out the moments that turned us off to learning and trusting.

Whenever I speak, I ask my audience to close their eyes and think of that teacher that had a profound effect on their life. What was it about that teacher that captured and inspired them to do their best? As this book will indicate, I truly believe that it is impossible to teach a child before you first capture and inspire that child. The special relationships that exist among teachers, students, and administrators are the keys that unlock the door to success and excellence in any school at any level.

On the pages that follow, you will become familiar with a recurring theme, one that will rekindle that flame in you that was once there or keep your flame burning strong as you struggle to educate one of America's most challenging generations.

***

Let me say a few words about this generation. As educators, you know how much competition we face to reach today's youth: everything from reality television to video games to MTV, VH1, BET, and the seductive back-beat of the Hip-Hop culture (more on this in Chapter 6). The conflict came home to me at a recent education conference where I was the keynote speaker. Speaking to the issue of this generation's dreams and aspirations, a teacher rose and said, "Everybody wants to be a pro athlete or a rap star. Even the four foot-two youngster thinks he is going to make it into the NBA."

These unreal dreams catch fire every time an eighteen-year-old signs a $90 million shoe endorsement contract. Every child lacking the grounding of an everyday role model—a parent or teacher or coach—feels that he or she might become the next sensation. Again and again, I wonder to myself: "Whatever happened to realistic dreams? Whatever happened to goals that you can achieve?"

Like so many boys, I, too, dreamed of being a professional basketball player when I was growing up. I spent countless days and nights practicing and perfecting my skills on the court. And my work ethic carried me to the first team of my conference's all-region team. I'll never forget the thrill I felt at being named one of the five best players in our region. It was such an honor!

I ended up receiving a full scholarship to play college basketball. But, like most of the young men who play college ball, I did *not* get drafted into the pros and ended my career having never stepped foot onto an NBA court.

I shared this story with a large group of inner-city teen-agers and, after completing my speech, one of the young participants approached me and said, "That was a good speech, but if I were you, I would leave that last part out." Both his mother and I laughed, knowing which part he was alluding to. I asked for a moment with him and shared that the last part is what I truly wanted him to hear.

Were I a young man today, one of the five best players in my conference, I'm sure I would have been tempted by the thought: "If I'm this good, maybe I should skip college and go straight to the pros." Back in my day, such a thought was nonsense—skipping college was neither encouraged nor expected. And what indeed would I have done if I hadn't received that college degree? My present career, my happy family life—none of these things would have been possible.

Our young people need to know that the best-laid plans do not always come true. We need to impart to them that they should dream, but make sure they have a back-up plan or two! Let's impart to them the importance of opportunity wedded to vision. That is, being a rap star is a beautiful vision, but a limited one. Obtaining a solid education creates opportunities for them to *own* the record company or *produce* the music. As educators let's not discourage their love of sports, but encourage them instead to dream about *owning* the professional sports team instead of hoping and praying to be offered the opportunity to play on one.

Fortunately for me, my parents taught me to dream realistic dreams and I did make receiving my college degree a priority. My family consisted of six children and all six of us went to college. It was an expectation in our home. There was not plenty of money coming into our door, but there was plenty of love and there were high expectations.

I recall those days so fondly now. My older brothers were exceptional basketball players, and my twin sisters were both smart and outgoing. I was the "baby" in this clan, and while I know now that my mother and father struggled to put food on the table and keep the lights on, at the time I was insulated from their worries.

How different are the problems of the current generation. Today, we have *children* working to help keep the lights on and food on the table when, at their tender ages, they should be concentrating on their dreams and aspirations and making good grades.

But to continue with my story, I recall the many good role models I had during my youth—my sister Jennifer, for example. From girlhood, she always "had a plan." She graduated in the top of her high school class and then went on to college where she again graduated at the top of her class.

She repeated that performance in law school, graduating again in the top of her class. Today she is the chief judge in one of the cities in our home state of South Carolina, while my sister Gale has become one of the best teachers I know. Jennifer and Gale always inspired me. They had vision and purpose, but knew their plans would take time and diligent effort. They then put *in* that time and effort in to making their dreams come true.

And then there were the teachers. To this day, I remember the way these men and women taught, how receptive I was to their instruction. The teachers of that generation *lived* to be teachers—put their whole heart and soul into their jobs. They never accepted failure from their students. To them, "Failure was not an option," and parents were their willing and eager partners in creating success for each child.

Finally, I think of the example that my mother set for me. Indeed, as she laid on her deathbed, she reminded me of the power of teaching and learning. She said, "No matter how good you are at sports, you must always have an education to rely on, to fall back on."

With all these models and mentors to guide me, at the crossroads of my life—when I was not drafted to go to the pros—my disappointment quickly gave way to the realization that my divine purpose was not becoming a professional basketball player, but becoming someone who would *capture, inspire* and *teach* our youth. From that moment forward, I never looked back with regret but only forward with anticipation of what was to come next.

As my trip down memory lane demonstrates, times have definitely changed. But rather than sighing for the good old days, we educators need to change with these times. There are many things we must do differently to have even a chance to reach this generation of children.

The first part of this book—"Student Perspectives"—lets us into the world of four teen-agers, some of whom are "problem" students, some of whom are not. I conducted many more interviews than just these four, and the things that most concerned this broad range of students provide an important backdrop for the individual experiences that I highlight.

Students told me:

- *Their schools are too big*
- *Some teachers really don't care*
- *Some of the students are just too "bad" to be taught*
- *Parents should be involved before their children get into trouble*
- *Principals should be careful about who they hire as teachers, coaches, teacher's assistants, etc.*
- *There should be more extracurricular activities for students*
- *Teachers should be more involved in extracurricular activities*
- *Students should get to know other students—even if they don't want to—through organized activities sponsored by the school*
- *Schools should not forget to bring people in to motivate the students*
- *Schools should show teachers the neighborhoods the students come from*

- *Students should be asked to be part of "the solution"*
- *Schools should develop traditions that mean something special to the students and teachers*
- *Schools should show students they really care about them*
- *Schools should reach out to parents and make them feel comfortable in the schools*
- *Schools should be consistent when enforcing rules*

The second part of this book—"What Every Teacher Needs to Know"—opens with a case study of one teacher whose entire classroom practice was shaped and transformed by his experience dealing with a "difficult" student. The succeeding chapters present issues that may not have been in the course materials in your college of education, but that every teacher must master in order to be successful.

Remember: The greatest contribution that we can make is to ensure there is a teacher in every classroom who cares that every student, every day, learns and grows and feels like a valued, important human being. We can be those teachers if we listen with our hearts to the voices of the children we encounter and embrace the simple tools outlined in this book.

Part I:

Student Perspectives

Chapter 1

Keisha

Born into the home of a single mother and six siblings, Keisha came into this world with the deck stacked against her. When she entered kindergarten, she noticed her teacher was warm and loving and always smelled "clean," as Keisha phrased it.

And she also noticed the differences and similarities between and among the other children in her class. One thing that made a major impression on her was the fact that some of the other children seemed happy all the time, an emotion she couldn't share. She wanted badly to be able to smile and have fun like the other children in her class, but it was hard to do.

"I always worried about mommy and if she was OK today and how she would make it through the day," Keisha recalls. "She seemed tired all the time. We were always running around, making noise and stuff, knowing our apartment wasn't big enough for us to run in."

TV, she says, was always a great escape. "We would get ideas of what kind of life we wanted to live by watching others on TV and seeing it in magazines."

In addition, "School was one of my favorite places because the same things happened every day. I always knew what to expect," Keisha says.

In Keisha's elementary school, children felt the love and concern the teachers and others had for them. On a daily basis, Keisha felt she had adults that truly cared about her. It made her wish the school day was longer.

When Keisha entered middle school, things began to change for her and not for the better. Her elementary school was a neighborhood school, and most of the children who attended the school were children who lived near her. Some of the teachers even attended her grandmother's church, so it was relatively easy to establish trusting relationships. Middle school required her to get on a bus and ride across town to attend school with children from a variety of backgrounds, races, and socioeconomic statuses.

She had more trouble establishing trust with her teachers; she questioned whether the teachers even cared for her.

Keisha was a ninth-grader when I interviewed her:

Q: *How do you feel about school?*
A: It's too crowded and we have too many fights. The profanity is out of control, but the adults can't seem to get them to stop. Bottom line is: I don't like it and don't feel safe in it.

Q: *What are your dreams for the future?*
A: I want to do hair and eventually open my own salon. I can also sing, so I might do something with that if the chance comes around.

Q: *How do you feel about your teachers?*
A: Most of them I don't care for 'cause they don't care for me. Some of them do things that make it clear to students that they don't really care about us. There are two of my teachers from last year that I like and respect. They treat me like I'm a real person and like I can be somebody if I

try hard. They also carry themselves like they are special. Those other teachers don't have no business teaching nobody's children.

Q: *Who is your favorite teacher? Why?*

A: Ms. Logan. She goes out of her way to make sure we understand what she's teaching us. She is more concerned about whether we understand than what we make on her test. Sometimes she will have us retake the test after she feels like we understand better. She makes learning fun! It's almost like a trick. Before you know it, she has everybody in the class working. We take lots of field trips too, which makes learning easier because we get to see what she is going to teach us about before she starts. That makes sense to me!

Ms. Logan told all of us on the first day of school that we all had A's in her class. Then, the next day, she had the Logan roll on her wall. Everybody in the class's name was on the Logan roll and next to our name was A. That's the first time since I started school that I saw my name on the wall with an A next to it. I wanted to keep it, so I worked real hard in her class to keep my A. At the end of the semester, I ended up with my first A on my report card. Ms. Logan made me feel like I was the smartest student she ever had. Yeah, she's my favorite teacher and that's why!

Q: *How do you feel about your principal and vice-principal?*

A: I don't usually see my principal a whole lot. They have a lot of phone calls to make and stuff. My vice principal is pretty cool. She is usually in the hallways and cafeteria during the day. They mostly deal with discipline all day long. That's got to be a tough job.

Q: *Who would you want to teach your younger sister or brother? Why?*

A: I would want Ms. Logan to teach my brothers and sisters. She makes you feel like you can do the work and get good grades on it. She also makes learning fun in her class. Other teachers seem like they are tired of teaching.

Q: *What would your "dream school" be like?*

A: We would have lots of activities and people would get along, no matter where they come from or what color they are. We would get help with our homework or subjects we have trouble with and pass those special tests that everybody gets so tensed about.

Q: *What would it take for you to go into a classroom every day, sit down and do your work?*

A: I already do this in some of my teachers' classrooms. They demand respect. I can't explain it. It's like, I wouldn't even think about acting up in their classroom. They give respect, too. In other teachers' classrooms, it's like having a substitute. You can do whatever you want to do because they are intimidated by some of the students. Sometimes, if our teachers came to school real confident that the lesson they planned would be interesting and exciting, our class would go smoother. [But] they want us to do these worksheets that are both boring and not related to what we're supposed to be learning and expect all to be well. Not going to happen. They have to make learning fun!

Q: *What are the three most important things ALL teachers should know?*

A: Most students do want to learn. We have a whole lot to deal with outside of school and we need respect, structure, and consistency.

Chapter 2

Marvin

"LET ME JUST sleep in class, and I won't bother you" was Marvin's motto until he met Mrs.Clanton in 8th grade. Marvin had been socially promoted so many times that he felt he had a right to sleep in class, but she was different from any other teacher he had known. She made him want to stay awake.

Mrs. Clanton had news for Marvin, and the news would take some time for her new student to digest. She was interested in him; she *wanted* to reach and teach him. Marvin found himself looking forward to going into Mrs. Clanton's class. He and his friends would talk about her: the exciting projects she had them doing, how she would make them feel like they were the smartest students in the world.

Marvin had never had anyone tell him he was smart before. But we teachers know that students rise to expectations. I can remember as a seventh-grader having a teacher who thought I was smarter than I was so I actually became smarter! Really! She would walk by my desk each day and whisper to me, "You're so smart." That teacher's book was always the first to come out of my book bag after school. I don't think I ever missed one of her homework assignments, not to mention studying for her tests. I wanted to show her that she was right about me.

But back to Mrs. Clanton. She had a reputation in school for being liked and respected by most of the students. She was always organized and always well-dressed. It was almost as if she felt she needed to "uphold" the profession. I found out later that she had been "captured and inspired" by a teacher who had those same qualities when she was a student.

Mrs. Clanton put Marvin on a weekly progress report, and she rewarded him at the end of each week that he made adequate progress. Now the goals were achievable. "Progress" might mean Marvin came to school all five days that week, which was a major accomplishment for him. Marvin had a bad reputation in school—most of the students were afraid of him. And while, on some level, it must have given him pain, he also gained pleasure from this.

But this disconnected, discontented student was beginning to like Mrs. Clanton's class and found himself staying awake more and more as she made the learning relevant and meaningful to him and his classmates. Class discussions were suddenly interesting, and she made the students part of the lesson. Mrs. Clanton was a master at forming positive relationships with her students. Her students bragged that she hadn't written a single office referral so far this school year. They actually took pride in the fact that they had something to do with that.

Marvin is the middle child in a family of four. His mother is the sole provider for the family and works long hours: 7 a.m. to 3 p.m. at one job and 4 p.m. to 11 p.m. at a second job.

Because his mother is working most of the time, Marvin has free reign in terms of how he wishes to spend his time. And he spends a lot of time watching TV. This jibes with current research, which tells us that, on average, a teen-ager watches six to seven hours of TV per day. That's almost the equivalent of a full-time job. Add to that a steady diet of violent, sexy, trashy video games and you have a recipe for trouble—trouble in our public schools.

Marvin's positive experience with Mrs. Clanton paved the way for other positive and caring relationships with teachers to develop. One of the most important for him was his relationship with Coach Anderson. They connected on the playing field and developed a healthy respect for each other. Marvin's dad was not in the picture at home, so the situation was a good one for him. Coach Anderson became the first adult to tell Marvin he was going to do something or be somewhere at a certain time. Even more importantly, Marvin actually obeyed. It's a thing that sounds so simple, but is huge in a developing child's mind, especially one who has been let down time after time after time.

After a period of time, Coach actually became an extended family member in Marvin's life—someone he felt comfortable sharing things he normally wouldn't have had anyone to talk to about. Research shows and common sense confirms the critical influence that an adult male presence has in helping youths transition from boyhood to manhood. Because of the respect he developed for Coach, many of Marvin's choices and decisions came to be based on the internal compass of: "What would Coach think/do/say?"

Marvin now had a guiding conscience in his life, something so many of our young men and ladies lack. Thank goodness for educators like Coach who are willing to become what our young students need them to become to save their lives.

By the way, at the time I conducted this interview, Coach Anderson had recently attended a student awards program where Marvin, for the first time in his life, received an award—for being the most improved student for the grading quarter.

Here are Marvin's responses to my questions:

Q: *How do you feel about school?*
A: I like school better this year than any other because I am more prepared to do the work. When I wake up in the

morning, it's hard to get motivated to come to school, but people like Coach Anderson make you want to come and do it for him even if you don't feel like doing it for yourself.

Q: *What are your dreams for the future?*
A: To become a pro football player and buy my momma a house and tell her she can quit her jobs. That's what I dream about all the time.

Q: *How do you feel about your teachers?*
A: Some of them are cool. Coach Anderson is the coolest, even though he don't take no stuff. Everybody knows he cares about them because of all the stuff he does for you like give you rides home from after-school tutoring and stuff like that. He came to my little brother's basketball game the other day.

Some of the other teachers act like they are scared of you, and others act like they don't like you because you from the 'hood. They make me angry 'cause they don't know what we got on our minds when we come to school. People like Coach seem to understand what the deal is. Maybe Coach grew up in the 'hood.

Q: *Who is your favorite teacher? Why?*
A: Next to Coach who isn't my teacher-teacher, I would have to say Mrs. Simmons. I looked up in the stands one Saturday morning at one of my football games, and there she was—sitting there. She told me she was going to come see me play, but I didn't believe her. Adults be telling you anything sometimes just to get you out they face.

I thought that was nice of her to come. I ran a touchdown and she was happy for me. The next week, I studied for her social studies test and passed it. We been cool since then. I didn't know Mrs. Simmons would know what a touchdown was! She also stayed after school when other children needed extra help or needed to make up a test or quiz. Other teachers would just give you a zero.

Q: *How do you feel about your principal and vice-principals?*

A: I don't like none of them and they don't like me. If it wasn't for Coach, they would've put me in the alternative school already. Nobody likes those dudes. They always acting all bad like they the president or something. If I ever became a principal, I think I would remember these dudes and try not to be like them. Are they going to read this? (Laughter)

Chapter 3

Vanessa

VOTED THE "most outgoing and cutest" her junior year in high school, Vanessa entered her senior year not knowing whether she was going to graduate. Most of her time centered around social events and hanging out at the mall, at movies, or wherever the "in crowd" happened to be gathering.

Vanessa grew up in a family with eight children and is the oldest in the family. She has been popular in school for as long as she can remember—and she's gotten in a lot of trouble because of this popularity.

As time to graduate approached, Vanessa began to realize how many opportunities she missed to take advantage of her gifts. Many of her teachers attempted to guide her in the right direction or at least away from those people, places and things that could ultimately bring her harm, but so many times she refused to listen.

Vanessa had always had a curiosity about life, and her social studies teacher in middle school recognized this and capitalized on it as she believed in supplementing straight textbook work with exposing her students as much as possible to the "real life" elements of what she would be teaching.

When Vanessa developed an interest in the civil rights movement of the 1960s, Mrs. Livingston found ways to stimulate her young student to the degree that Vanessa had at least five questions a day related to this subject.

She ended up with an A in the class and a new-found respect for her teacher. The experience with Mrs. Livingston taught Vanessa that she could easily apply herself to something she found interesting. This experience would prove critical in her life.

But when Vanessa moved on to high school, she fell back into her old ways: the socializing, popularity contests, parties, and so on. Her report card reflected her lack of interest in her studies. Vanessa actually enjoyed getting up in the morning and attending school, but for all the wrong reasons. School to Vanessa was a social ground, like the mall.

As Vanessa sat quietly in her senior guidance counselor's office waiting for the session to determine her graduation status to begin, she began asking herself, "Where has all the time gone? It seemed like yesterday that I was in elementary school, and now I am getting ready to graduate from high school and enter a world that holds no promises and gives you nothing."

Vanessa reflected on all the "good times" with her friends and thanked God for the fact that she was not pregnant or a mother like so many of her friends. Their lives were not their own any longer as the babies they had required all of their energy and time.

Many of their dreams had been destroyed by their choices. But there was still time for her to figure out her future—this was Vanessa's conclusion as Mr. Harvey entered the room to discuss her senior status.

Q: *How do you feel about school?*

A: From the earliest time I can remember going to school, I've always liked it. But, not for the work. I like it because I get to see my friends every day and hang out. I also like the extra activities that go on after school like the football and basketball games.

Q: *What are your dreams for the future?*

A: I want to go to college and go into hotel management or something like that. I like being around people and planning events for them. My guidance counselor is helping me with locating schools that have good programs in this area.

Q: *How do you feel about your teachers?*

A: Most of them are cool. They have a lot to deal with at school with the students being the way they are today. They don't have any respect for teachers so, that's got to be hard for them to deal with every day. Some of them really care.

Q: *Who is your favorite teacher? Why?*

A: My middle school teacher, Mrs. Livingston. She was like a mother at school and didn't take stuff from anybody. She made learning fun, and we understood what she was trying to teach us because she exposed us to it before she tried to teach it. That made it better for all of us. We respected Mrs. Livingston a lot, and she wanted us to make something of ourselves.

Q: *How do you feel about your principal/vice-principal?*

A: I don't really know my principal. We don't see a whole lot of him. I see my vice-principal in the cafeteria and he works real hard at school. Our school is big, and I'm not sure what the principal does after the announcements. I see a lot of parents in our school that he has to meet with, I guess. My principal in elementary school used to talk to me a lot in the cafeteria. I used to see her every day. I guess it's different being a principal in elementary school versus high school.

Q: *Who would you want to teach your younger sister or brother? Why?*

A: Mrs. Livingston, because she always made me feel safe and like I was the smartest student in the classroom. I always looked forward to being in her classroom and didn't want to leave to go to my next class. I would want my younger sister and brother to have an experience like I had with her as my teacher. She taught us like we were her own children.

Q: *What would your dream school be like?*

A: Full of teachers like Mrs. Livingston, lots of extracurricular activities, and students and parents who care about the school. It would also be safe and free of bullies.

Q: *Who is the best teacher you ever had? Why?*

A: My sixth grade teacher, Mr. Malloy. He made sure we learned something every day and never made us feel like we couldn't master the work he gave us. I gained a lot of confidence in myself from being in Mr. Malloy's class. He would call your house and tell your mom about good things you did at school. He did this more than once, and I appreciated that so much because my mom didn't play around when it came to school. I believe he is still teaching today. We need more teachers like him.

Q: *What would it take for you to walk into a teacher's classroom, sit down, and pay attention?*

A: The class would have to be important. Most teachers that are liked by the students don't have to worry about this. It's the teachers that students don't like that have classrooms where students misbehave and don't pay attention. There's not a lot of learning going on in these classrooms because the teachers spend most of their time writing referrals and sending students to the office.

Q: *What are the three most important things all teachers should know?*

A: To respect their students, be well prepared, and have high expectations of their students.

Chapter 4

Tyrone

A STAR ATHLETE, good looking, charming. This was Tyrone's image among his classmates, especially the girls. Tyrone's attendance was good because he liked being in the social environment that school afforded him. He also liked the praise he received from being a star basketball player at his high school. Indeed, Tyrone received so much support from his school, one would find it hard to determine who was a family member and who wasn't. School has been the place where Tyrone has always found security, commitment, and love.

An eleventh-grader at the time I interviewed him, Tyrone had one year of eligibility left and then he'd move on to play college basketball somewhere. But while there were numerous colleges and universities interested in him as an athlete, his grades were not consistent throughout the school year. Tyrone did well enough to maintain his eligibility during basketball season, but as soon as the season was over, his G.P.A. dropped considerably.

Several of Tyrone's teachers spent extra time trying to make sure he did his part. And Tyrone was well aware that he has an opportunity no one else in his family has had: an opportunity to go to college. Though only 16, he felt burdened by the weight of trying to make sure he gets his family out of the 'hood and into a better environment.

Tyrone would be happy just to get out of the two-bedroom apartment that has been home to him, his five sisters and brothers, and mother for the past sixteen years. Many of Tyrone's dreams revolved around this scenario. His favorite daydream was that he finished high school, accepted a scholarship to play basketball in college, finished college, got drafted into the NBA, then helped fulfill all of his family's hopes and dreams.

At night when he lay down to go to sleep, he was consumed with the pressure he felt to get his family out of its present socioeconomic condition. This pressure is in no way an exception among many of our youth today. Education has always been and continues to be the springboard out of poverty for families, but many of them fall short of the goals they set for themselves by dropping out before graduation or not advancing further after it.

For Tyrone, timing is everything. He has a lot going for him and the key question facing him is, "How is he going to discipline himself to compete at a higher level, academically and athletically?"

Tyrone responds to my questions:

Q: *How do you feel about school?*

A: School has always been a cool place for me. I don't like all the work the teachers put on students sometimes, but most of my experiences have been pretty good. Things are changing in a lot of ways because the teachers are different and the students are different. Most of the time you have to watch your back, and that is exhausting. By the time you focus again, you've missed an important assignment or failed to study for a test or exam.

It's hard to keep your focus these days. My uncle told me when he went to high school, the worst thing that could happen to you is you might get into a fight and get beat up at school. Things are a lot different in school now. If you make a mistake and step on someone's shoes, you could get shot. That is not exaggerating. So, school is cool most of the time.

Q: *What are your dreams for the future?*

A: From the time I was a little boy, I always dreamed of playing pro basketball. I have seen a lot of good players go to college and not make it so, I try to make sure I do well enough in school to finish and get my degree. This way, I will have something to fall back on. We had a guest speaker about a month ago, and his story was something like mine. I paid close attention to what he was saying because I wanted to find out what happened to him in the end. He never made it to the pros, but did finish college and now he owns his own company. That's cool to me. If I don't make it, which I know I will, then I hope to finish college so I can get a good job and take care of my folks.

Q: *How do you feel about your teachers?*

A: I have a couple of teachers that are real cool. They understand students and the changing times. The other teachers here are stuck in a time capsule. They don't know what's happening. They still believe in threatening to call your mom, not knowing that most of the students could care less if they call or not. They seem to let the students get next to them, like, agitate them. I like the teachers who think it's funny when we stress out and stuff like that. They don't pay enough money to go through what most teachers go through. I couldn't do it for what they make. I kinda feel sorry for some of them sometimes. Then, I don't feel sorry for some of the others because they bring it on themselves.

Q: *Who is your favorite teacher? Why?*

A: I would have to say Coach Tally. Even though he teaches me health and is also my basketball coach, he is the best. He is always prepared. You can tell he spent time putting together what we are going to do in the classroom and on the court. He also has a lot of respect for students and they respect him, too. I don't think I've ever seen him send a student to the office. I've seen him get upset now! Most of the students like him and respect him. He treats you special.

Q: *How do you feel about your principal/vice-principal?*
A: Our school is so big, I hardly ever see my principal or vice-principal. We have deans that take care of discipline and lunch duty and stuff like that. If you ask half the students, they might not be able to tell you who the principal is at our school.

Q: *Who would you want to teach your younger brother/ sister?*
A: I would want Ms. Burke and Mr. Wiggins to teach my sisters and brothers. They teach you stuff that's hard, but in a way you understand it. All the students that had these teachers seem to do well in everybody else's class because they teach you all you need to know to do well in other classes. Most of the students in our school really respect these two teachers. They care about the student as a person, so it goes beyond what subject they teach you. I can't count how many of my games these two teachers attended. It seemed like they were always there. That meant a lot to me because I know teachers are tired after they deal with us all day.

Q: *What would your dream school be like?*
A: My dream school would be safe and clean. It would serve breakfast in the morning and give students a lot of choices for lunch. Teachers would be nice, and students would want to go to this school. We would have a winning football and basketball team and have lots of pride about

going to our school. We wouldn't have a lot of over-age students. Students would pass to the next grade when they are supposed to, and we would help younger students get used to our school when they first come.

Q: *Who is the best teacher you ever had?*

A: My fourth grade teacher, Mrs. Brown, was the best teacher I ever had. She never missed a day of school. You could count on Mrs. Brown being at school every day, and she knew where we lived. She used to come by our house to tell my mom I was good at school. I used to think that was strange, but I like the ice cream Momma would give me as a special treat for being good at school. My classmates used to call me teacher's pet because if I left my lunch money or didn't have lunch money, which was more the case, Mrs. Brown used to buy me lunch. I probably owe that lady five hundred dollars for paying for my lunch all those days. She didn't seem to mind. She just wanted to make sure her little bright minds had the energy to think, she would say. Our classroom was always full of bright colors and sunlight. She would display our work all over the place so others would be as proud as she was of us. I really wish Mrs. Brown could have taught me throughout my school days. She made you feel like you could learn anything. She was that good.

Q: *What would it take for you to go into a classroom every day, sit down, and do your work?*

A: This would be hard to do every day. Most of the time, you have to go in and do your work or you will fail the class, but all students have to be able to take a break at some point and chill. Some of those lessons take you into overdrive. That's when I usually start writing notes or finding out where the parties are for the night or weekend. I try not to be disrespectful to the teacher, but some students don't care about that part. They just do what they do. It also matters who the teacher is because, in some teachers' classrooms, you can't chill at all. They will not let you.

Q: *What are the three most important things ALL teachers should know about students?*

A: Students really do care whether they pass or fail no matter what they say or do. Some students are afraid or too embarrassed to say they don't understand something in front of their classmates. They would rather fail. And students are looking for the connection of what the teacher is trying to teach to why do I need to know this.

Part II:

What Every Teacher Needs to Know

Chapter 5

Deposits and Withdrawals

JONATHAN GREW up in a hard-working middle-class family. With a mother and a sister who were teachers, Jonathan always knew that he, too, would be a teacher. As a youngster, he'd listen to all of the stories about school and the children his mother encountered daily. As he went through high school and college, Jonathan tried to pick up tips from each of his teachers and professors. He was excited about the profession and determined to be the best teacher in the world.

Jonathan met Keisha during his first teaching assignment out of graduate school, at an inner-city high school teaching ninth grade English. Keisha was in his first period class. And he felt the momentum gathered through his childhood dreams and all the courses he took and passed with flying colors come to a screeching halt against the brick wall of her attitude.

None of his graduate school courses mentioned students like Keisha. Jonathan felt he could have used a course just on her attitude. When the second day of school was no better than the first, Jonathan was quick to ask some veteran teachers for help, only to hear the response, "If you find something that works, please let us all know."

Was it a mistake to take this job? he asked himself. Should I have gone to a more affluent school system where the students behave better and understand the importance of respect and education?

After several negative encounters with Keisha, her cousins, and friends, Jonathan got a break. He made a simple decision to volunteer as a chaperone at one of the school dances. Everyone in the community looked forward to the Friday night school dances. But as the night approached, Jonathan wondered whether he'd made another mistake by signing up to help out.

Arriving thirty minutes early, he was able to chat with some of the tenured teachers at the school, and he was surprised by the positive comments many of them shared about their experiences with the children, the community, and the parents of some of the students.

He realized that, as the new kid on the block, he had been surrounded at school both by teachers who were as green and overwhelmed as he was and by unhappy teachers who truly wanted out but had no place else to go. Their negativity had been bringing him down, but this Friday night dance conversation was appealing and encouraging.

The night would get much better!

As Jonathan helped Cathy, the vice-principal, put the last punch bowl on the table he began to feel a part of a team for the first time since beginning his new profession. He finally felt that he made the right choice by becoming a teacher. One of the veteran teachers shared an important tip with Jonathan, telling him that many of the most important exchanges that take place between a student and teacher take place outside of the classroom. He went on to state that after that first positive exchange takes place, many in-class exchanges could follow.

As soon as Jonathan began to relax, the doors to the gym opened and students started pouring in—chattering, shouting, laughing. Jonathan felt his confidence begin to sag once again until Keisha called out to him: "Hey teach, you go get your groove on tonight?"

He had no idea what she was talking about so he just replied, "I'm here to help tonight."

"All right, teach, see ya later," she smiled and moved on with her friends.

The night flew by with the fast songs. And Jonathan learned to separate the students dancing too closely or dancing inappropriately during the slow songs.

Before he knew it, the dance was over, and many of the students were thanking Jonathan for coming. "That was nice—something to build on," he thought. But on the way home, Jonathan couldn't get Keisha and her friends out of his mind. They seemed so different at the dance than they did in the classroom.

Educators have always known that relationships play a big role in making positive things happen in a school or building. But, since 1980, we have concentrated our energies and efforts in schools on achievement and higher test scores. We use so many different approaches to teaching, dissecting it and discussing it endlessly. Yet we seldom seem to recall that the most important part of teaching and learning is directly related to the relationship that exists between the teacher and the student.

When one asks students who have struggled most of their lives how they got a break and successfully made it through college and into the middle class, the answer is always connected to a relationship with a teacher, coach, or counselor who took an interest and created a positive relationship with them.

Stephen Covey (1989) uses the notion of an emotional bank account to convey the crucial aspects of relationship building. In all relationships, he argues, one makes "deposits" and "withdrawals."

Deposits	Withdrawals
Seek first to understand	*Seek first to be understood*
Keeping promises	*Breaking promises*
Kindness, courtesies	*Unkindness, discourtesies*
Clarifying expectations	*Violating expectations*
Loyalty to the absent	*Disloyalty*
Apologies	*Pride, conceit, arrogance*
Being open to feedback	*Rejecting feedback*

Jonathan made a deposit when he decided to chaperone the school dance, and Keisha and all of her friends noticed it. One seemingly unimportant choice would become the catalyst for a whole new group of positive relationships with his students. From the night of the dance throughout the first semester of school, Jonathan noticed that not only was he able to teach his classes without stopping to send students to the office, he was actually getting students to complete assignments and study for his tests.

Jonathan realized early in the year that his coursework in school could never have prepared him for the demands his students made on him. This is not to denigrate teacher education in any way: There will always be a need for coursework and pedagogy, but equally important is the need to connect with students and create relationships with them built on reciprocal respect.

Take, for example, a school that has a policy that bars students from wearing hats inside the building. And let's say Marvin, the disconnected and disaffected student from Chapter 2, walks in one day with a hat on. What is the impact if the principal says, "Take that hat off! You know you're not supposed to have that hat on in this building"? The rude tone creates a hostile environment. Now what if the principal had said instead, "Son, would you mind removing that hat, please?" Same scenario—two different ways of dealing with the situation, two different results.

The first response will, more times than not, result in the student's "going off," i.e., losing control and cursing the principal, especially if this is all playing out in front of his peers. The second way saves face, as the principal is operating from a standpoint of reciprocal respect.

It sounds really simple, doesn't it? As Jonathan processed his encounters with his students, he realized he was sending students to the office less and less frequently. Was it the students or was it me? he asked himself.

The answer, quite honestly, was: It was both. Jonathan was beginning to create in his classroom an environment where he, as the teacher, could teach and his students could learn.

It is critical for the reader to understand the dynamics of how this occurred. Jonathan created the new climate inside his classroom by starting *outside* of his classroom. He learned to build strong relationships not only with his students, but with all students.

As Jonathan's first year of teaching ended, he was worn out and tired, but it was a good tired, one that left him feeling as though he had done something good for the world—and indeed he had.

Jonathan is entering his third year teaching and has volunteered to spend some time each year with a new teacher. This will be invaluable to the new teacher, especially to one teaching for the first time.

Jonathan has come to feel the rewards of working with his students are worth all the withdrawals they make from his bank account. He's even had some students make deposits.

Chapter 6

Waiting for Their Next Audition?

WHEN I ASK young people, as I always do, "Where do you see yourself at 20 years old?" I can always be assured that, among the many responses they offer, someone is going to say: "I am going to be rich and famous." We teachers are attempting to educate a generation of students who have their eyes fixed on a different kind of prize than we are accustomed to, and we are finding it increasingly difficult to win the race.

We teachers push the idea and importance of learning: college, graduate school, law school, medical school. But *America's Next Top Model*, *The Bachelorette*, *The Real World*, and all the rest send a much more seductive message: That the opportunity for that "fifteen minutes of fame" has been extended to an opportunity to become rich and famous. We continue to preach, but our children are saying, "Why?"

What they fail to realize is that these shows are selling a fantasy, not "the real thing." The percentages of those that fail to "make it" are very high. And for those that do succeed, seldom do our young people have the opportunity to see the trials encountered, the obstacles that had to be overcome.

The unreal and incomplete images of success are extremely damaging to youth because they make it harder for them to live life on life's terms. The inevitable disappointments leave them wide open for the risks of abusing drugs, alcohol, sex, and other substances associated with escaping reality.

From an adult, middle-class perspective, it's easy to see the effects of not achieving an education. But so many of our children cannot. It has become increasingly difficult to make a case for education when children are surrounded by images of easy money and other material things acquired simply by writing lyrics and adding a beat or playing a little boy's game.

But even this becomes a "teachable moment" for us. As educators, we must make a relevant case. We can stress the fact that talent requires far more perspiration than inspiration to flower. We can teach young people that they must know the essentials of reading, writing, and arithmetic even if they become sports stars—so that they'll know which contract to sign and which not to.

We cannot blame our young people for chasing fame and fortune when they live the way they live on a daily basis. In 2004, according to the latest estimates from the U.S. Bureau of the Census, 12.7 percent of the nation's 296.4 million people were poor—defined as an income below $9,645 for an individual or $19,307 for a family of four. Bureau statistics also reveal that:

Poverty Differs Across Groups

- The poverty rate for all persons masks considerable variation between racial/ethnic subgroups. Poverty rates for blacks and Hispanics greatly exceed the national average. In 2004, 24.7 percent of blacks and 21.9 percent of Hispanics were poor, compared to 8.6 percent of non-Hispanic whites and 9.8 percent of Asians.
- Poverty rates are highest for families headed by single women, particularly if they are black or Hispanic. In 2004, 28.4 percent of households headed by single women were poor, while

13.5 percent of households headed by single men and 5.5 percent of married-couple households lived in poverty. In 2004, both black and Hispanic female-headed households had poverty rates just under 40 percent.

- There are also differences between native-born and foreign-born residents. In 2004, 17.1 percent of foreign-born residents lived in poverty, compared to 11.8 percent of residents born in the United States. Foreign-born, non-citizens had an even higher incidence of poverty, at a rate of 21.7 percent. In total, the foreign-born poor account for about a sixth of all poor persons.
- Children represent a disproportionate share of the poor in the United States; they are 25 percent of the total population, but 35 percent of the poor population. In 2004, 13 million children, or 17.8 percent, were poor. The poverty rate for children also varies substantially by race and Hispanic origin.

Family Characteristics of Low-Income Children

Parental Employment

- 55% of children in low-income families—15.9 million—have at least one parent who works full-time, year-round.
- 27% of children in low-income families—7.8 million—have at least one parent who works part-time or full-time, part-year.
- 19% of children in low-income families—5.5 million—do not have an employed parent.

Parental Education

- 26% of children in low-income families—7.7 million—live with parents who have less than a high school education.
- 35% of children in low-income families—10.3 million—live with parents who have only a high school diploma.
- 38% of children in low-income families—11.2 million—live with parents who have some college or more.

There are important cultural and behavioral differences between the poor, the middle class, and the wealthy. For an indispensable guide to understanding these differences and bridging the communication gap, I highly recommend Dr. Ruby Payne's *A Framework for Understanding Poverty*.

The picture painted by the statistics and Dr. Payne's book will be familiar to any teacher of urban youth, who sees whole families of many generations—mothers and grandmothers, sisters and brothers—mired in want, dreaming of the day they'll be rescued. Young children feel pressured to save their families from poverty; Some of them are even forced to become the providers in their families.

And then society then places added pressure on them by telling them they need to wear $150 sneakers and jeans to fit in—and guess what? Our children believe it! And in the process, they turn school into a social place where they go to wear their new "gear," compare prices, and see who has the "hook-up" and who doesn't.

I'm reminded by this discussion of a Michigan State University study that compared family life in the U.S. during the decades of the '50s, '80s and '90s. The study highlighted changes in the five major influences on our youth: home, church, school, peers, and television.

The decade of the '50s seems like another world. There were clear rules and schedules. Families consisted of a father, mother, and children. At six o'clock, most families sat down for dinner. Conversation at the table revolved around "How was your day?"

Home was the No. 1 influence on a child. And without distractions like television, video games, rap music, etc., reading was an important pastime for adults and children. Books opened us up to new worlds that we didn't know existed. And they had another benefit: Schools did not have high percentages of students enrolled who couldn't read on grade level.

The second major influence on children of the '50s was church. To this day, I can recall learning so much in church and developing and keeping such a respect for the institution. Church was the place many of us learned the difference between right and wrong. The loss of structure, as the church influence has faded, has caused many of our problems in school today.

School was the No. 3 influence on children's lives during this period. I'll speak at some length about how different our schools were at this time. The subjects of reading, writing, and arithmetic were the key elements that drove instruction. Teachers were able to teach their students because most of them came to school ready or at least willing to learn.

Most teachers lived close to the school where they taught, thus becoming a part of the community in which they taught. Children not only saw their teachers in school, but also in the community and in church, too.

According to those who were in school at this time, teachers were highly respected and so was education. Students saw the connection between education and the future lives they would lead.

Peers came in fourth on the list of influences—followed by television, which featured shows like *Lassie*, about a dog who helped people. I watched that show as a boy at my grandmother's house. My grandmother would have a heart attack if she were alive today to see the sex and violence that permeates television programming today.

In the 1950s, television came in dead last among influences on children—today it is No. 1.

Dr. Payne notes that television provides an important escape but we educators know—because we see it in our schools every day—how high the cost is. The youth of the past worried that a teacher might call their parents to complain about something that occurred at school. The youth of today are worried about living another day. Under the influence of television, they have come to believe that the most important elements in our society today all have to do with what is on the outside: beauty, money, fame, cars, houses, and jewelry.

How can we, as educators, use this to turn our children on to inner values, such as learning? The most important thing is to begin by placing quality individuals in front of our children on a consistent basis. Those in the decision-making capacity to hire teachers, support staff, and administrators have a new responsibility to put the best in front of the best.

In the end, the question should always be, Will these teachers teach these children the same way they would want their biological children taught?

When we start with such a question, there is a new element of accountability, not to be confused with the kind we seek with test scores and other measures of higher achievement.

If an adult is willing to deliver teaching and love to students at the same level that they wish these things delivered to their own children, this may not solve the scenarios that exist in urban schools, but I promise you, it's a great start.

Chapter 7

"My Teacher Doesn't Like Me"

"Our greatest contribution is to be sure there is a teacher in every classroom who cares that every student, every day, learns and grows and feels like a human being."

As I ENGAGE with my audiences during workshops or training sessions, one of the main discussion points is always the personal investment the teacher makes in the student. I always ask the question, "Do you teach each of your students as if he/she was your own biological child?"

The response is almost always a collective gasp, indicating that this is an *aha!* moment. Isn't this what we all are supposed to do when we are given the awesome task and responsibility of educating our youth and arming them with life skills?

In my conversations with students, almost always they tell me they have teachers who simply do not like them.

Well, let's be honest about this issue. Teachers are human, too, and, quite frankly, students today are very challenging, to say the least. So, how do we address the critical issue of liking, students who return, with interest, the dislike they say they feel daily from their teachers?

Those of you who have read my work or heard me speak before know how important I feel it is to develop a special relationship with each student in order to truly teach that student. In the absence of such a relationship, such a special connection, it's almost impossible to ensure success with students.

But there are many barriers to creating those connections. Many of my student interviews report how frustrated teachers seem to be. *"SEEM?"* is usually my response to that feedback. I've noticed the frustration, too, and it's greater than ever before, not because of one or two specific causes, but a multitude of pressures teachers and administrators face daily.

Teachers are struggling to keep up with stringent state accountability measures, plus the federal "No Child Left Behind" legislation. At the same time, children are not coming to school ready to learn. Some are not even willing to learn.

What can schools do? What can teachers do? And is there anything at all that can be done if it's true that teachers don't like the students?

To be perfectly honest, I believe there is some truth to that feeling among students. Children feel things with their spirits—they know whether one is sincere or not sincere. It can be very difficult to fool a child—they know!

In addition, I've worked in schools in many capacities, I travel the nation visiting schools as a consultant, and, yes, I've seen with my own eyes that there are *some* teachers working in schools every day *who do not like children.* Despite that fact, for whatever reason, they return each year when school begins, and those who are in a position to stop them from coming back, for whatever reason, are not exercising that option.

It is extremely important that those of us in a position to place adults in front of children do so with prayer, proper guidance, and wisdom. Teachers have the power and authority to help create dreams or break them, to build up a child or destroy her.

Let me be clear: I believe the majority of teachers who teach do so from their hearts and souls and give everything they have to see to it that their children's lives are better as a result of the exchange of knowledge and experience. But, again, there are those out there who ruin the experience for everyone else.

The majority of us are continuously telling young people, "We really, really care about you." But the uncaring teachers create huge trust issues.

Those of you who know the high-poverty urban population of children know that trust is not a word in their vocabulary. Because they have been let down by so many adults in their lives, it makes it difficult to believe in other adults, particularly those who are not even family.

The question arises, "Why do you care?"

Indeed, it's a good question. If anyone should care, it should be family, after all. When children are let down over a consistent period of time by family, it becomes difficult to believe anyone else really cares about them or their well-being. And it's confusing to a child when someone outside that circle expresses caring.

Another critical issue here is, once you get or earn their trust, what do you have to do to keep it or sustain it?

First and foremost, you must be honest. The first time you get caught in a lie, even a small one, guess what? It's over for good. I have always found that children are resilient and can handle the truth. It's lies that break them.

So how can a teacher gain the trust of a child who is "difficult"? The most effective way is to spend time with those students outside of school. Attend their baseball or soccer games or awards banquets. Show them that you care by showing up on your time, not the school's time.

As the old saying goes, "Action speaks much louder then words." Children respond more strongly to the nonverbal cues than to all the words in the world. It makes a powerful impression on them to see a teacher making time outside of work for them.

When teachers show up at a student's baseball, soccer, basketball, or football game on a weekend, you better believe they know you were there. It helps to relay the message to them that we care about them beyond the classroom, that we care about them as people.

Teachers must understand the power of forming positive relationships with their students and the results these relationships bring. It is so much better to invest time and energy up front developing these special relationships than it is to not develop them and end up spending the better part of your day writing discipline referrals.

Now I am not saying for one moment that once you develop positive relationships with your students that you will no longer write office referrals. But I am saying with conviction you should not have to write as many.

A teacher might say: "I can accept my good students, those who behave and do good work, but I can't accept those who do not work, who have the wrong attitude, and who cause me trouble."

That teacher has forgotten that it's the acceptance of *all* students that gives power to the teacher. In fact, it is in relation to students who are difficult that the teacher's true qualities are demonstrated.

We all find it easy to accept those who lend themselves to our designs. It is in their relationship to those who cause them trouble, who are dirty and poorly dressed, and who fail to achieve that teachers prove their bedrock values.

It is the essence of the point of view presented here that only a complete gift of oneself makes the teacher an artist. Teaching is a jealous profession; it is not a sideline.

This is not only because of the problem of time, nor because of the impact of lesser efforts on pupils: It is because of the effect on the teacher himself.

It is only as we give fully of ourselves that we can become our best selves. Thus halfway measures and attitudes of whatever kind reduce our effectiveness.

When we ask teachers to give themselves fully to their students, to their colleagues, to their communities, and to humanity, we are thus only asking them to be maximally effective. Moreover, it is only as the teacher gives himself that she or he can experience completely the joys and satisfactions of the profession.

In this situation the teacher is in the same position as any artist. Frustrated artists are often those who for one reason or another are unable or unwilling to make a complete gift of themselves to their art. Similarly, the unhappiest teachers are those who bemoan the weaknesses of their students and the conditions under which they work and fail to sense that it is their own half-hearted efforts that defraud them.

One measure of the teacher's willingness to give lies in his accessibility to his students, his willingness to spend time with them. One difficulty here is the narrow conception that often prevails about what it means to teach.

To teach means more than to lecture or explain before a group of students. The best teachers influence their students more in their personal, individual contacts with them than in strict classroom situations.

If teaching and learning are complementary processes, if the teacher is to teach by learning and if his teaching is to be directed toward an individual, she must know that individual. And how is she to know that individual if she spends little or no time with her students except in the classroom?

Another illusion limits us. It is the illusion that there is some magic in lecturing and in the hearing of recitations. We want as much time for this as possible. We begrudge taking time to work with individual students. Yet we know very little about the actual effectiveness of what we do.

Is it not at least possible that our classroom work would be greatly increased in effectiveness if only we spent more time with our students as individuals? We seem to be obsessed with teaching. But at heart we know that no one can educate another person, that all of us educate ourselves. The teacher's role is that of a helper in the process.

The question is: How can we best help?

One of the best ways we can help is to understand better how we interact with our students on a daily basis. How do we approach them? What do we say to them? How do we say it? What about our body language? What are we shouting without even opening our mouths that might negatively affect our students and our ability to teach them?

Yes, I'm talking about nonverbal communication.

It is not only *what* you say in the classroom that is important, it's *how* you say it that can make the difference to students. Nonverbal messages are an *essential* component of communication in the teaching process, especially, experts like Ruby Payne tells us, among children of families living in poverty for whom nonverbal communications are far more important than verbal.

Teachers should be aware of nonverbal behavior in the classroom for three reasons:

1. *An awareness of nonverbal behavior will allow you to become better receivers of students' messages.*
2. *You will become a better sender of signals that reinforce learning.*
3. *This mode of communication increases the degree of the perceived psychological closeness between teacher and student.*

Some major areas of nonverbal behavior to explore are:

- Eye contact
- Facial expressions
- Gestures
- Posture and body orientation
- Proximity
- Humor

Let's consider each of these at greater length:

Eye contact

Eye contact, an important channel of interpersonal communication, helps regulate the flow of communication. And it signals interest in others. Furthermore, eye contact with audiences increases a speaker's credibility. Teachers who make eye contact open the flow of communication and convey interest, concern, warmth, and credibility.

Facial expressions

Smiling is a powerful cue that transmits:

- Happiness
- Friendliness
- Warmth
- Liking
- Affiliation

If you smile frequently, you will be perceived as more likable, friendly, warm, and approachable. Smiling is often contagious and students react favorably and learn more.

Gestures

If you fail to gesture while speaking, you may be perceived as boring, stiff, and unanimated. A lively and animated teaching style captures students' attention, makes the material more interesting, facilitates learning, and provides a bit of entertainment.

Even as small a gesture as a head nod communicates positive reinforcement to students and indicates that you are listening.

Posture and body orientation

You communicate numerous messages by the way you walk, talk, stand, and sit. Standing erect, but not rigidly so, and leaning slightly forward communicates to students that you are approachable, receptive, and friendly.

Furthermore, interpersonal closeness results when you and your students face each other. Speaking with your back turned or looking at the floor or ceiling should be avoided; it communicates disinterest to your class.

Proximity

Cultural norms dictate what is a comfortable distance for interaction with students. You should always be on the lookout for signals of discomfort caused by invading students' space. Some of these include:

- Rocking
- Leg swinging
- Tapping
- Gaze aversion

Typically, in large classes space invasion is not a problem. In fact, there is usually too much distance. To counteract this, move around the classroom to increase interaction with your students. Increasing proximity enables you to make better eye contact and increase the opportunities for students to speak.

Humor

Humor is often overlooked as a teaching tool, and it is too often discouraged in high school classrooms. But laughter releases stress and tension for both teacher and student. You should develop the ability to laugh at yourself and encourage students to do the same. It fosters a friendly classroom environment that facilitates learning.

Obviously, adequate knowledge of the subject matter is crucial to our success with students; however, it's not the only crucial element. Creating a climate that facilitates learning and retention demands good nonverbal and verbal skills. To improve your skills, record your speaking on videotape. Then ask a colleague to suggest refinements.

Of course, we can't leave the topic of communication without discussing the impact of what we say. We can invite students in—or disinvite them—just as easily with our words as with our deeds.

The following lists of inviting and disinviting verbal comments have been identified by educators and students as indicators of the quality of life in schools. These lists are only illustrative, but the presence or absence of items on theses lists may help to identify the stances taken by those who lead or work in and around your school. These items may also serve as a checklist for schools that are already doing good things and want to do them better.

Inviting Comments	Disinviting Comments
Good morning.	*Keep out.*
Thanks very much.	*What are you doing?*
Congratulations.	*Use your head.*
Let's talk it over.	*It won't work.*
How can I help?	*Call me back.*
Tell me about it.	*You can't do that.*
I appreciate your help.	*I don't care.*
Happy Birthday!	*Not bad.*
I enjoy having you here.	*Don't be stupid.*
I understand.	*How are you?*
We missed you.	*He can't be.*
I'm glad you came by.	*Stay home.*
I like that idea.	*That's stupid*
I think you can.	*No way.*
Welcome.	*Closed.*
I like what you did.	*It's OK.*
Welcome back.	*Oh, boy!*
You are unique.	*Who's calling?*
That's even better.	*Needs more work.*
I've been thinking of you.	*What's your name?*
How are things going?	*I don't have time.*
How are you?	*Excuse me.*
I'd like your opinion.	*Write it down.*
Happy holiday!	*Whatever!*
What do you think?	*Why do you come?*

Chapter 8

Capture, Inspire, Teach

I BELIEVE STRONGLY in a three-step process to teaching and learning. Looking back over my twenty-plus years of experience in education, I always come back to this conclusion.

A teacher must capture a student before he or she can teach that student. In addition, the student must also be inspired. Someone must be standing in front of them in a credible way with something to share that they are interested in receiving.

The first step, the capturing process, is all about developing, establishing, and sustaining positive relationships with students that can carry over from year to year. The second step, inspiring students, is equally important in order to get to the ultimate goal of teaching and learning.

In all of my interviews with students, they have always shared with me the importance of having someone in front of them to motivate and inspire them to want more. This is so important and cannot be underrated.

The third and final step is to teach.

Teaching used to be a noble profession. One could count on being proud if there was anyone in the family who was a teacher. It's amazing the respect they had years ago and how the reputation of the profession has eroded.

My three-step process allows teachers, classroom, and schools to change the emphasis from "No Child Left Behind" to "No Child Left Out."

Over the years, I have found that successful schools rely upon relationships that have been established and maintained with the children in those schools. Books and the information contained in them are very important, but mean very little if the student is not interested in receiving what's in between the pages.

And what motivates students to open themselves to what's between the pages of books? Relationships! It all hinges on positive *relationships*! It's just that simple. Everything else follows.

So let's explore further the characteristics of successful schools and school systems.

1. They all have a *common vision or mission* and everyone who works in or with the school knows what it is. What happens, however, if only 20 percent of teachers, school level and central office administrators, parents, students, and support staff actually know what the mission statement is? This is a document that's supposed to be the driving force behind everything a school stands for and attempts to do for children. How can it be a driving force if no one knows what it is? Schools that are adrift need to take a look at their guiding documents and develop more meaningful, purposeful mission statements.

2. They all have *quality leaders*. Note I did not say managers; I said leaders. There is a difference. This is not to say that we don't need quality managers, because we do. But leaders understand people and know how to get the best out of them. They know where to assign them and where not to. They are experts in affirmation and validation. They are also

child advocates, secure, knowledgeable, and healthy in spirit, body, and emotions.

3. *Students come first* in these schools/systems. This is, after all, why we're all here.

4. They have a *quality professional development plan* which the teachers/staff have helped to design. Because of the level of input, everyone feels ownership.

5. *Continuous improvement* is a common thread: Everyone is trying to get better.

6. There are *positive relationships* as well as encouragement and support. The students and adults in these buildings understand the importance of support and respect. They actually speak to each other.

7. There is *synergy* to accomplish team goals by coming together as one entity with one mission.

8. There may be *parental involvement/support*. This is always a plus but not always present. Many parents want to be involved but because of work schedules, etc., they find it difficult.

9. *Everyone understands their roles*, from administrators, teachers, and support staff to students. And the expectations are clear and realistic.

10. *Failure is not an option.* The energy exerted in these schools is focused on "success." Conversations, actions, and reactions are solely geared to this goal.

I want to say a word about the climate that adults create in the schools. There should be a minimum of bickering present among the adults, a "biggie" for those of you who work in our schools.

The adult climate in each school should be relaxed, yet serious. A professional demeanor should always be a priority as should an attitude of success. Adults in successful schools with good school climates understand their specific and general role in their respective schools. They also understand that their children come first, and they are the only reason the school exist in the first place.

It's funny sometimes to walk into a faculty lounge and hear questions such as: "Why does Billy even come to school?"

Billy comes to school because he expects you to teach him! How about that for a reason?

And then there's the issue of the student climate—and frankly, it's impossible for a school to succeed or even operate properly if there is a problem in the student climate.

Students need clear expectation. They should all understand that teaching/learning comes first. And while there are many activities in the school for the students, participation in these activities is not a given.

Students have to earn the right to participate and to continue to participate. There are standards to live by and these standards must be upheld consistently.

As teachers, we will from time to time encounter difficult behaviors in the classroom. I offer the following to assist with certain troubling behaviors. Please note these are offered as suggestions and may not work in all situations.

The student is rambling, wandering around and off the subject.
- *Refocus attention by restating relevant point.*
- *Direct questions to group that is back on subject.*
- *Ask how topic relates to current topic being discussed.*
- *Use visual aids, begin to write on board, turn on overhead projector.*
- *Say: "Would you summarize your main point please?"*

The student is shy or silent, afraid or unwilling to participate.
- *Change teaching strategy from group discussion to individual written exercises.*
- *Give strong positive reinforcement for any contribution.*
- *Involve by directly asking him/her a question.*
- *Make eye contact.*
- *Appoint the student to become a group leader.*

The student is too talkative, a know-it all, manipulator, or chronic whiner.
- *Acknowledge comments made.*
- *Give limited time to express viewpoint or feelings and then move on.*
- *Make eye contact with another student and move toward that student.*
- *Give the student individual attention during break or at the end of class.*
- *Say: "That's an interesting point. Now let's see what others think."*

We must always remember, the better our relationships with students, the lower the number of classroom interruptions and challenges we'll face. Research shows that 90 percent of a school's discipline problems stem from 10 percent of their student population.

This tells me that our classrooms are manageable, especially when we begin to capture those in the 10 percent.

Our children await you!

Chapter 9

Nobody Rises to Low Expectations

BECAUSE OF my family background, school has always been a central element in my life. And looking back, elementary school was by far the most interesting period of my education.

That statement may be surprising. But when I think those years, I think about teachers who never accepted failure. Who, when you had finished a school year and moved on to the next grade, automatically knew who your last teacher was. Who seemed to put their stamp on you. My, how things and times, children, and teachers have changed.

I recall expectations always being high as we moved from subject to subject, assignment to assignment. I didn't always feel smart, but felt like I could hold my on against any of the other students. And, indeed, I was often the last one standing in the Friday spelling bees in Mrs. Beaton's class.

Then in seventh grade, junior high school, as we called it then—I encountered the best teacher I have ever had. I discovered during this time that I was smarter than I gave myself credit for being.

To put it another way: My teacher thought I was smart, smarter than I thought I was, so I rose to her expectation.

Isn't that interesting? She made me feel smart all the time. She would walk by my desk every day and whisper, "You're so smart."

WOW! Whose book do you think I pulled out of my book bag first when I would get home from school in the afternoon? Whose tests do you think I studied for a little harder than the others? I wanted to hear her say those words over and over again. It gave me incentive to do my best.

Here's another important thing to note about Mrs. Black: She went the entire school year without writing an office referral. She didn't need to, as most of her classroom discipline came from the other students in the class.

Nobody wanted to ever see Mrs. Black in an uncomfortable situation. That is how much students liked and respected her. She not only understood her students, she understood the general principles of motivation.

Basic principles of motivation exist that are applicable to learning in any situation. And if you learn them, you'll be on your way to a stress-free classroom like Mrs. Black's.

> 1. *The environment* can be used to focus the student's *attention* on what needs to be learned. Teachers who create warm and accepting, yet businesslike, atmospheres in class will promote persistent effort and favorable attitudes toward learning. This strategy is successful in children and in adults. Interesting visual aids, such as booklets, posters, or practice equipment, motivate learners by *capturing* their attention and curiosity.

> 2. *Incentives motivate learning.* In a general learning situation, self-motivation without rewards will not succeed. It can be difficult for children to find satisfaction in learning based on the achievement of a long-term goal that is useful to them—it's even less common for them to be motivated by the pure

enjoyment of exploring new things. But *privileges* and *praise* offered by a teacher who has thought about the incentive that is likely to motivate an individual at a particular time will *inspire* students every time.

3. But having said that, I must also note that *internal motivation is longer lasting* and more self-directive than external motivation, which must be repeatedly reinforced by praise or concrete rewards. Unfortunately, children of certain ages and even some adults have little capacity for internal motivation and must be guided and reinforced constantly. The use of incentives should be based on the principle that learning occurs more effectively when the student experiences feelings of satisfaction. Caution should be exercised in using external rewards when they are not absolutely necessary. Their use may be followed by a decline in internal motivation.

4. *Motivation is enhanced* by the way in which the instructional material is organized. In general, the best-organized material makes the information meaningful to the individual, either by relating new tasks to those already known or by determining whether the persons being taught understand the final outcome desired and instructing them to compare and contrast ideas.

5. Finally, *learning is most effective* when an individual is *ready to learn*, i.e., when she wants to know something. Sometimes the student's readiness comes with time, and the teacher's role is to encourage its development. But if it's urgent that a desired change in behavior occur, the teacher may need to supervise directly to ensure that the change

happens. If a student is not ready to learn, he or she may not be reliable in following instructions and, therefore, must be supervised and have the instructions repeated again and again.

A word of warning. None of the techniques will produce sustained motivation unless the goals are realistic for the learner. The basic learning principle involved is that *success is more predictably motivating* than is failure.

Ordinarily, people will choose activities of intermediate uncertainty rather than those that are difficult, in which they perceive little likelihood of success, or even easy, in which they perceive a high probability of success. For highly desired goals, there is even less tendency to choose more difficult conditions. So allowing learners to assist in defining the goals increases the probability both that they will understand them and that will want to reach them.

Of course, students sometimes have unrealistic notions about what they can accomplish. We touched on this in our discussion of unrealistic dreams in Chapter 6. Often, the student does not understand the precision with which a skill must be carried out. Alternatively, they may not have the depth of knowledge to master some critical material.

To identify realistic goals, teachers must be skilled in assessing both student readiness and student progress toward goals. Here are a few things to keep in mind as you set about the task of helping your students to set and achieve their goals.

The Role of Anxiety

Because learning requires changes in beliefs and behavior, *it normally produces a mild level of anxiety*. Mild anxiety is good—it's useful in motivating the individual. However, severe anxiety is always bad—it's incapacitating.

Now there are some educational situations in which a high degree of stress is inherent. But if an individual's level of anxiety gets too high in those situations of stress, the individual's perception of what is going on around him grows limited and his ability to perform is hampered.

In those situations, teachers must be able to identify the source of the anxiety and understand its effect on learning. They have a responsibility to avoid one source of severe anxiety in learners: setting unrealistically high goals for them.

But the goals must be set because, without them, there can be no growth. They should be set, moreover, for each student, and feedback should be provided regarding progress toward the goals.

Perhaps you're groaning to yourself, "This sounds like and is a lot of work." It is. Just remember that goal-setting demonstrates an intention to achieve and activates learning in your students from one day to the next. It directs the student's activities in a purposeful way and offers them an opportunity to experience success. And what did we say about success at the beginning of this discussion? Success is more predictably motivating than failure.

The Role of Affiliation and Approval

Affiliation and approval are strong motivators.

It's human nature to seek out others with whom to compare abilities, opinions, and emotions. Affiliation can also result in direct anxiety reduction through the mechanisms of the social acceptance and, oftentimes, the mere presence of others.

However, these motivators have a down side—they can lead to mindless conformity, unhealthy competition, and other negative behaviors.

A Framework for Thinking About Motivation

We must recognize that no grand theory of motivation exists. But motivation is so necessary for learning that strategies should be planned to organize a continuous and interactive motivational dynamic for maximum effectiveness.

Of course, an enormous gap exists between knowing that learning must be motivated and identifying the specific motivational components of any particular act. But we can say two things with certainty: 1) that the general principles of motivation are interrelated; and 2) that a single teaching action can use many of them simultaneously.

Recognizing these facts, we teachers must focus on learning the patterns of motivation that apply to an individual or group, realizing that errors will be common.

It is in that spirit that I offer the following framework for analyzing motivation factors and strategies.

At the Beginning of Any Learning Process	
Student Motivational Factors	*Teacher Motivational Strategies*
Attitudes: toward the environment, teacher, subject matter, and self	Positivity: make the conditions that surround the subject positive
Needs: including security, esteem, etc., within the learner at the time of learning	Challenge: confront the possibly erroneous beliefs, expectations, and assumptions underlying negative learner attitudes
	Planning: tailor activities to allow learners to meet identified needs
	Sensitivity: reduce or remove components of the learning environment that lead to failure or fear

In the Middle of Any Learning Process	
Student Motivational Factors	*Teacher Motivational Strategies*
Stimulation: note which learner intelligences are affected by the experience	Variety: change style and content of the learning activity
Affect: note the emotional experience of the learner while learning	Involvement: use problem solving, role playing, etc., to make learners essential to learning process
	Relevance: use learner concerns to organize content and develop themes and teaching procedures
	Collaboration: use team concepts to maximize learner sharing
At the End of the Learning Process	
Student Motivational Factors	*Teacher Motivational Strategies*
Competence: achieving this makes learners value the learning experience	Feedback: provide consistently regarding mastery of learning
	Acknowledgement and Affirmation: of the learner's growing skill
	Consequences: take advantage and make explicit natural learning situations
	Reinforcement: creates a feedback loop to stimulate more learning
	Closure: provide a positive ending to the experience

Chapter 10

Strategies for Urban Youth

THE FOLLOWING strategies are based on my twenty-plus years in education, working with schools that made great strides in a small amount of time. They are simple, time-honored tools that worked for me. I'm certain they will also work for you.

Base ALL of your interactions on reciprocal respect.
    Ask: "Would you mind removing your hat, please?"
    Don't issue orders: "Take that hat off!"

Use positive affirmations as much as possible.
    Don't just ignore the student's work.
    Say: "You are awesome! That was really good!"

Seek first to understand then to be understood.
    Say: "Explain that to me again, please. I want to be sure I understand what you are saying."

Realize that you may be the only steady, consistent force in your student's lives.
    Tell them, "I want you to know I am always here to help and support you in any way I can," and mean it!

Be consistent.
    Keep your word and always be on time.

Be fair.
    Listen to both sides of a dispute—don't prejudge or play favorites.

Be flexible.
Rules are guidelines, not prison chains.

Be compassionate.
Think of how you would want your own child to be
treated.

Be tolerant.
Remember what you were like as a child, your own days
in school.

Be human.
Remember that we are none of us perfect, no matter what
our age.

Be supportive.
It requires fewer muscles to smile than to frown.

Be open-minded.
If this a challenge with your current student population,
work on building those relationships. Good relationships
will help in this area.

Have high, but reasonable, expectations for all students.
Know them and their capabilities. Be careful not set them
up for failure, but at the same time hold them account-
able for an achievement level that is appropriate to their
abilities.

Assess and challenge.
Always know where your students stand academically,
then challenge them to go to the next level.

Be positive.
Tune out the negative put-downs by teachers who haven't
been as successful as you are going to be. Form your own
opinions about your students. Please!

Incorporate student ideas and suggestions into your classroom routines or daily practices.

This will help create a relationship based on reciprocal respect as students love to feel their ideas are valued.

Make students feel special that they are being taught by YOU!

What is it about YOU that separates you from a mediocre teacher? Your students should feel proud that they have this opportunity. They become more inclined to take advantage of opportunities they feel are special.

Be consistent with rewards and incentives—use them to create and build hope in your classroom.

Create an honor roll on the first day of school and give every student an "A".

This is how you begin school on a high note. Make it clear to them that it is now up to them to keep their names on the roll as the school year progresses. You will be amazed as to how seriously many of the students will take this. Many of them have NEVER seen their names on an honors list before.

Finally, LOVE YOUR CHILDREN and THEY WILL LOVE YOU BACK.

Every teacher should teach every child the same way they would like their own biological children taught. When teachers refuse this ideal, we betray our calling.

Afterword

As you process the words and pages from my book, I pray that you realize and accept the wonderful calling that governs your life. Teaching is one of the most wonderful professions one could choose.

I would like to leave you with a special tribute to our profession sent to me by an audience participant. This piece is so touching that I wanted to make sure it traveled from me to you.

The Teacher

There is a story many years ago of an elementary teacher. Her name was Mrs. Thompson. And as she stood in front of her 5th grade class on the very first day of school, she told the children a lie. Like most teachers, she looked at her students and said that she loved them all the same. But, that was impossible, because there in the front row, slumped in his seat, was a little boy named Teddy Stoddard.

Mrs. Thompson had watched Teddy the year before and noticed that he didn't play well with the other children, that his clothes were messy, and that he constantly needed a bath. And Teddy could be unpleasant. It got to the point where Mrs. Thompson would actually take delight in marking his papers with a broad red penstroke, making bold X's and then putting a big "F" at the top.

At the school where Mrs. Thompson taught, she was required to review each child's past records and she disliked

Teddy so she put his off until last. However, when she finally reviewed his file, she was in for a surprise.

Teddy's first grade teacher had written, "Teddy is a bright child with a ready laugh. He does his work neatly and has good manners . . . he is a joy to be around."

His second grade teacher wrote, "Teddy is an excellent student, well liked by his classmates, but he is troubled because his mother has a terminal illness and life at home must be a struggle."

His third grade teacher wrote, "His mother's death has been hard on him. He tries to do his best, but his father doesn't show much interest, and his home life will soon affect him if some steps aren't taken."

Teddy's fourth grade teacher wrote, "Teddy is withdrawn and doesn't show much interest in school. He doesn't have many friends and sometimes sleeps in class."

Mrs. Thompson felt deeply ashamed of her behavior when she read these notes. Then Christmas came, and she felt even worse. The students brought her presents wrapped in beautiful ribbons and bright paper—except for Teddy's. His present was clumsily wrapped in the heavy, brown paper he got from a grocery bag.

Mrs. Thompson took pains to open it in the middle of the other presents. Some children started to laugh when they saw the gift: a rhinestone bracelet with some of the stones missing and a bottle that was one-quarter full of perfume. But she stifled the children's laughter when she exclaimed at how pretty the bracelet was, put it on, and dabbed some of the perfume on her wrist.

Teddy Stoddard stayed after school that day just long enough to say, "Mrs. Thompson, today you smelled just like my Mom used to." After the children left she cried for at least an hour.

That was the day Mrs. Thompson quit teaching reading, writing, and arithmetic. Instead, she began to teach children.

She paid particular attention to Teddy. As she worked with him, his mind seemed to come alive. The more she encouraged him, the faster he responded. By the end of the year, Teddy had become one of the smartest children in the class. And the lie that she had told, that she would love all the children the same, became truth as she found she loved Teddy, too.

A year later, she found a note under her door, from Teddy, telling her that she was still the best teacher he ever had in his whole life.

Six years went by before she got another note from Teddy. He then wrote that he had finished high school, third in his class, and she was still the best teacher he ever had in his whole life.

Four years after that, she got another letter, saying that while things had been tough at times, he'd stayed in school, had stuck with it, and would soon graduate from college with the highest of honors. He assured Mrs. Thompson that she was still the best and favorite teacher he ever had in his whole life.

Then four more years passed and yet another letter came. This time he explained that after he got his bachelor's degree, he decided to go a little further. The letter explained that she was still the best and favorite teacher he ever had. But now his name was a little longer—the letter was signed, Theodore F. Stoddard, M.D.

The story doesn't end there. You see, there was yet another letter that spring. Teddy said he'd met this girl and was going to be married. He explained that his father had died a couple of years ago and he was wondering if Mrs. Thompson might agree to sit in the place at the wedding that was usually reserved for the mother of the groom.

Of course, Mrs. Thompson did. And guess what? She wore that bracelet, the one with several rhinestones missing. And she made sure she was wearing the perfume that Teddy remembered his mother wearing on their last Christmas together.

They hugged each other, and Dr. Stoddard whispered in Mrs. Thompson's ear, "Thank you Mrs. Thompson for believing in me. Thank you so much for making me feel important and showing me that I could make a difference."

Mrs. Thompson replied: "Teddy, you have it all wrong. You were the one who taught me that I could make a difference. I didn't know how to teach until I met you."

The author of this story is unknown. But it makes me remember conversations from my past, things that were said and done by people whom I thought would be with me forever. These times remind me of what I used to read about, what I now think and pray about.

Never before have I felt more strongly that education is the way to be peaceful, free, and productive. But how do we let the children know?

These times remind me of the voice I hear, so soft but so powerful, prompting me to tell my story, urging me to ask you to listen. If we spent as much time listening as we do talking, we'd learn so much more, we'd have so much more to give.

In these difficult times, we must all learn to give more and love more than ever before. This is our mission and our calling.

> Our children *need you.*
> Our children await you.
> Do *you* know enough about them to teach them?

Suggestions for Further Reading

Covey, Stephen R.
The Seven Habits of Highly Effective People.
New York: Simon & Schuster, 1989.

Cunningham, Patricia M., and Allington, Richard L.
Classrooms That Work.
New York: Harper/Collins, 1994.

Kozol, Jonathan.
Amazing Grace: The Lives of Children and the Conscience of a Nation.
New York: Crown Publishers, 1995.

Kunjufu, Jawanza.
To Be Popular or Smart.
Chicago: African American Images, 1988.

Payne, Ruby.
A Framework for Understanding Poverty.
Texas: RFT Publishing Co., 1998.

Purkey, William.
Inviting School Success.
Wadworth, 1984.

Other Titles by Stephen Peters:

Inspired to Learn: Why We Must Give Children Hope.
Atlanta: Rising Sun Publishing, 2001.

The Gentlemen's Club Curriculum Guide.
The Peters Group, 2002.

Do You Know Enough About Me to Teach Me? Teacher Workbook: Specific Strategies for Working With Urban Youth.
The Peters Group 2004.

The Ladies Club Curriculum Guide.
The Peters Group, 2006.